A School Concert

By Heather Hammonds

I think our school should have a big concert at the end of the year.

School concerts are fun for everyone.

Every child in our school can be in a big concert.

The teachers help the children plan the program.

The parents, grandparents and friends come to the concert.

They are very happy when they see their children trying their best.

The older children
put on a play at the concert.

They make the costumes
and paint the masks.

The younger children
dance and sing together.

They try hard not to forget
their dance steps
or the words of the songs.

Some boys and girls
from the gymnastics club
put on a display.

Their parents like to watch them.

A school concert at the end of the year is a very happy time.